# DOUGLAS
## TO
# RAMSEY
### including the Foxdale branch

## Tom Heavyside
*Series editor Vic Mitchell*

**MP** Middleton Press

*Front cover picture: Beyer Peacock 2-4-0T no.11 **Maitland** makes a spirited departure from Sulby Glen while returning to Douglas from Ramsey in July 1967. (D.J.Mitchell)*
*Back cover picture: This is described in caption 37.*

# ACKNOWLEDGEMENTS

In addition to those mentioned in the photographic credits, I would like to record my gratitude to P.Abell, P.Atkins, M.Bairstow, N.Bennett, M.Bishop, C.P.Boocock, R.Carter, M.Casey, R.M.Casserley, G.Coltas, Ms S.Cooil, A.Corlett, G.Croughton, R.D.Darvill, M.Farr, J.Fozard, Rev P.Frear, C.Goldsmith, E.Gray, R.Herbert, D.A.Kelly, Mrs A.Kennaugh, D.Kennaugh, C.Kenyon, S.Lace, S.Lambie, B.C.Lane, T.Nall, H.Phillips, N.J.Pinder, D.T.Rowe, K.Smith, G.Stacey, and I.Watson. Also to the staff at the Manx Museum Library in Douglas and Manchester Central Library. Reproduction of the gradient profile and items of ephemera are by kind permission of Manx National Heritage. I am indebted too, to R.K.Hateley who drew the map of the island and the station track plans and to P.Abell and D.J.Mitchell for reading through the proofs. Again, my sincere thanks to everyone.

*Published August 2004*

*ISBN  1 904474 39 X*

*© Middleton Press, 2004*

*Design        David Pede*

*Published by*
> *Middleton Press*
> *Easebourne Lane*
> *Midhurst, West Sussex*
> *GU29 9AZ*

*Tel: 01730 813169*
*Fax: 01730 812601*
*Email: info@middletonpress.co.uk*
*www.middletonpress.co.uk*

*Printed & bound by Biddles Ltd,Kings Lynn*

# INDEX

I. Map of the Isle of Man showing the railway network.

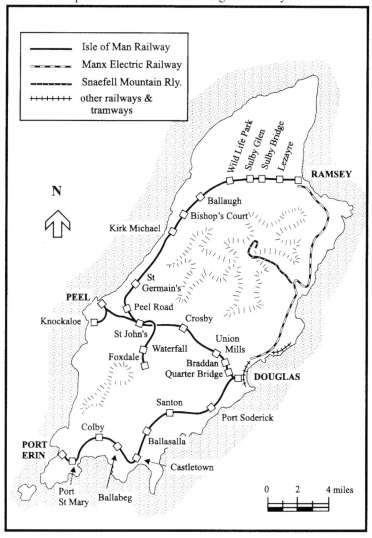

II. One inch to 1 mile Ordnance Survey map 1920 edition. Apparent is the circuitous route taken by the line so as to avoid the Northern Upland Massif. The first part of the route appears in our *Douglas to Peel* album.

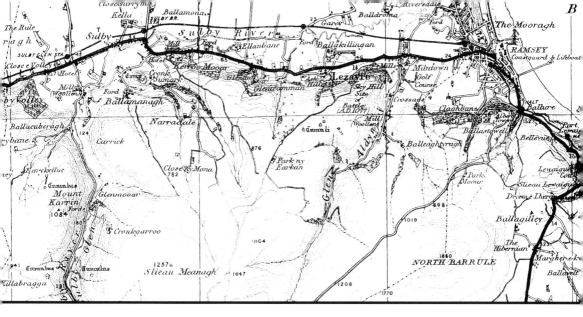

# GEOGRAPHICAL SETTING

The Isle of Man is encompassed by the Irish Sea and covers an area of approximately 227 square miles. In parts it is quite mountainous, the Northern and Southern Upland Massifs being separated by the narrow confines of the Central Valley. The northern range is also bounded by the Western Coastal Plateau and the Northern Plain.

Both Douglas, the most important port and capital of the island, and Ramsey, the main town in the north and the second largest on the island, are on the eastern seaboard. By the most direct road, which passes near to the summit of Snaefell, the tallest mountain on the island at 2,036ft above sea level, the two towns are some 15 miles apart.

However, from Douglas the railway first followed a westerly path through the Central Valley, staying close to the River Dhoo as far as Crosby and then the River Greeba (which feeds into the Dhoo) until it reached the summit of the line near Ballacurry crossing. The line then continued along falling gradients to St John's. Soon after leaving St John's the course of the railway changed to a northerly direction, with the section from St Germain's to Orrisdale, between Kirk Michael and Ballaugh, almost hugging the western coastline in places. From Orrisdale the line then headed east towards Ramsey, after Sulby tracing a path that was never very far away from the River Sulby.

Thus by threading the Central Valley, keeping close to the coast on the west side of the island and then following the edge of the Northern Plain the railway effectively skirted round the Northern Upland Massif. Throughout its 25-mile length it rested on a bed of Manx slate.

## Foxdale Branch

The branch was connected to the Douglas to Ramsey route some 250yds west of St John's station. From the junction, which faced Ramsey, the railway diverged a little to the north before burrowing under the St John's to Castletown road. It then curved sharply to the south and crossed over the Douglas line just to the east of St John's station.

The line then continued its incessant climb along the valley of the Foxdale River as far as the village of Foxdale. The river itself penetrates a little further towards the core of the Southern Upland Massif, the tallest peak in this range at 1,586ft above sea level being South Barrule, two miles to the south-west of Foxdale.

Like the Douglas to Ramsey route, the track was supported by an underlying layer of Manx slate. Around Foxdale there are also some rich deposits of lead ore.

# HISTORICAL BACKGROUND

When it was first formed, the Isle of Man Railway had intended to serve all the main towns on the island, but much to the chagrin of the people of the north the plans to include Ramsey were soon abandoned. The Douglas to Peel route duly went ahead as planned and was opened on Tuesday 1st July 1873, while services from Douglas to Castletown and Port Erin commenced during the following year on Saturday 1st August. The rails were laid to a gauge of 3ft 0in.

Thus it was left to a separate undertaking, the Manx Northern Railway, to promote a railway from Ramsey via Kirk Michael to St John's, where it was to link up with the IoMR metals. Construction work began in March 1878, with the inaugural public services starting, without the usual formalities associated with such occasions, on Tuesday 23rd September 1879. Unless otherwise stated, the intermediate stations north of St John's opened at the same time.

As an independent concern the MNR was destined not to survive very long, as it was absorbed by the IoMR on 19th April 1905. Thereafter, up until the start of World War II in 1939, the annual number of passengers carried by the IoMR ranged from a high of 1,609,155 in 1920 to a low of 603,676 in 1930, the figures much depending on the popularity of the island as a holiday destination.

Shortly after the end of World War II in 1945 tourists once again began to flock to the island in vast numbers, so much so that in 1947 the railway recorded 1,535,256 passengers. In many ways this proved a watershed insomuch that the general trend from then on was for the island to welcome fewer and fewer visitors each year. This, coupled with increased car ownership, had a serious impact on rail passenger numbers, with a consequent loss of income.

By the dawn of the 1960s, although still carrying over 900,000 passengers per annum, mostly during the Summer months, in a day to day context the IoMR was far less important to the island than in former years. Overall, it was in a rather run-down state and it became necessary to consider some stringent economy measures. One such was to withdraw the passenger service over the St John's to Ramsey route for the Winter period from October 1961 - the previous Winter the line from St John's to Peel had suffered a similar fate but in 1961 this stayed open. During the succeeding Winters the rails north of St John's were again closed to passengers, but then, after Saturday 13th November 1965, with very little prior warning, the whole of the IoMR network was shut down. Reputedly this was a temporary measure, the official announcement stating *to enable urgent track maintenance work to be carried out without interruption*. However, throughout the next year, 1966, and into 1967, the booking office windows remained firmly boarded-up.

As matters transpired it was the Marquess of Ailsa who instigated the reopening of the railway under a 21 year leasing arrangement. Amidst much pomp and ceremony public services were

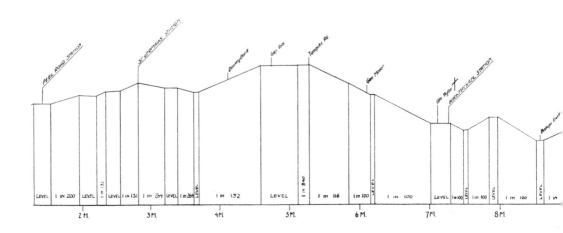

reinstated to the Douglas to Peel line for the Summer season on Saturday 3rd June 1967, while trains commenced running between St John's and Ramsey the next day.

Regrettably, as far as the line across the centre of the island to Peel, and that to the north were concerned, this was but a short-lived venture, for from 1969 Ailsa decided to confine his activities to the Douglas to Port Erin line. The last passenger trains over the St John's to Ramsey route ran on Friday 6th September 1968, while services along the Douglas to St John's section, which also served Peel, were concluded the next day. During the rest of that month an occasional oil train continued to operate from Peel to Milntown, near Ramsey, while up until 1971 stock was moved from time to time between Douglas and the carriage shed at St John's.

The track was lifted during the years 1974 to 1976, and after the Government had purchased the assets of the IoMR in 1978 most of the discarded routes were given over for use as footpaths, the section from Quarter Bridge to St John's (and on to Peel) now being known as the Steam Heritage Trail. However, on a more positive note, during the main tourist months, the stirring sight of a veteran steam locomotive can still be witnessed at Douglas before the start of yet another trip along the surviving section of the IoMR to Port Erin. This is now operated by Isle of Man Transport, whose headquarters at Douglas were relocated in 2000 to new offices built on the site of the old carriage shed, on the opposite side of the running line to the engine shed and workshops.

**Foxdale Branch**

The Foxdale Railway Co Ltd was registered on 16th November 1882 with a view to laying a 2½-mile branch from St John's to the village of Foxdale and gaining access to the lead mining area. Nominally an independent company, in essence it was very closely allied to the Manx Northern, most of the directors also being on the board of the MNR. In fact, the MNR were to operate the line.

An official opening took place on Monday 16th August 1886 (a small amount of freight having been carried during the previous two months), but within five years, in July 1891, the company had gone into liquidation. After this the MNR continued to operate the line on behalf of the liquidators until such time that it was taken over by the IoMR, along with the MNR, in April 1905.

From June 1940 the service was normally provided by a bus, as had some scheduled services in earlier years. After this, during World War II, the rails saw further usage by spoil trains and some troop specials, together with the occasional passenger train during the Summer months due to a shortage of buses. The last trains to use the branch were a couple of specials for the permanent way department in January 1960, sent to recover track materials from Foxdale station.

Thereafter the rails were left in situ for many years, not being recovered until the mid-1970s. As with the other closed lines on the island most of the route now provides a pleasant walkway.

III. Gradient Profile Peel Road to Ramsey.

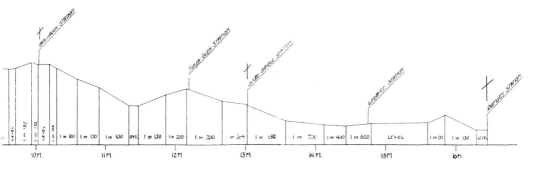

# PASSENGER SERVICES

The table below shows the number of trains running from Douglas to Ramsey each weekday, and on Sundays, during the peak Summer period and the Winter months in selected years from 1887. Normally, they were scheduled to stop at all stations although in some years an express was timetabled serving St John's, Kirk Michael and Ramsey only. Leaving Douglas the Ramsey line coaches were usually attached as far as St John's to a set destined for Peel.

|  | Summer | | Winter | |
|---|---|---|---|---|
|  | Weekdays | Sundays | Weekdays | Sundays |
| 1887 | 9 | 3 | 5 | 0 |
| 1897 | 10 | 3 | 5 | 2 |
| 1907 | 13 | 3 | 7 | 2 |
| 1917 | 7 | 2 | 7 | 2 |
| 1927 | 10 | 2 | 10 | 3 |
| 1937 | 11 | 3 | 7 | 0 |
| 1947 | 10 | 0 | 6 | 0 |
| 1957 | 5 | 0 | 3 | 0 |

In addition there was often a late evening service on some Thursdays, Fridays and Saturdays from Ramsey to either Ballaugh or Kirk Michael and return. Further, in later years, an early morning train ran from Ramsey to Kirk Michael, principally in order to provide a return working for the benefit of pupils attending school in Ramsey. It should be noted that some trains regularly ran as mixed formations with an array of freight wagons at the rear, this often necessitating some shunting while en route.

In 1967, after Lord Ailsa had assumed responsibility for the day-to-day operation of the railway, during the peak season there were three trains from Douglas to Ramsey on weekdays and one on Sundays. The section between Douglas and St John's was also served by a further eight trains which then continued to Peel. In 1968, as far as the line north of St John's was concerned, the service was somewhat limited, for even during the busy weeks of the season there was but one train from Douglas to Ramsey and back, and then only on Mondays, Wednesdays and Fridays.

## Foxdale Branch

Initially, from August 1886, the branch was served by five trains each way on Mondays to Saturdays, but the following year the service was reduced to four in Summer and two in Winter. In 1897, throughout the year, only two trains ran to Foxdale each weekday, thereafter the number varying between two and four.

April 1880

# LOCOMOTIVES

In January 1879, in anticipation of the opening of their line from Ramsey to St John's later that year, the Manx Northern Railway ordered two locomotives from Sharp Stewart & Co Ltd of Manchester. Like the Isle of Man Railway, whose slightly older Beyer Peacock-built nos 1 to 6 were already operating the lines from Douglas to Peel and Port Erin, the MNR opted for locomotives with a 2-4-0 wheel configuration fitted with side tanks. The engines, numbered 1 and 2, were transported to Ramsey that same year in time for the opening of the railway. Later, they were named *Ramsey* and *Northern* respectively.

The two MNR engines had 3ft 9in diameter driving wheels powered by outside cylinders measuring 11in diameter with an 18in stroke. Although these details were the same as the Beyer Peacock-built IoMR locomotives most of the other dimensions were quite different. For example, *Ramsey* and *Northern* had a total wheelbase of only 11ft 0in as against the IoMR engines 14ft 6in, and a water carrying capacity of 400 gallons - when built the tanks of IoMR nos 1 to 3 held 320 gallons and those of nos 4 to 6 385 gallons, while the bunkers could contain 1¼ tons of coal in comparison with the 14 cwt of IoMR nos 1 to 6. In full working order the Sharp Stewart engines turned the scales at 19 tons 0 cwt, a little heavier than their IoMR counterparts.

The following year, 1880, when the MNR required a third engine, rather than return to Sharp Stewart's, they accepted the tender from Beyer Peacock. No.3 *Thornhill* was constructed in their Manchester workshops at the same time as IoMR no.7. These two were identical to IoMR nos 4 to 6.

A few years later, when the MNR realised a much more powerful locomotive would be needed to handle the expected heavy loads of mineral traffic once the Foxdale Railway was open, they turned to the Glasgow-based firm of Dübs and Co. In 1885 they accepted delivery of the 0-6-0T no.4 *Caledonia* which had 13½in x 20in outside cylinders and 3ft 3in diameter wheels, with a total wheelbase of 10ft 9in. At the maximum boiler pressure of 140lbs per square inch it could generate 11,120lbs of tractive effort, more than double that of MNR nos 1 to

3. *Caledonia's* tanks held 480 gallons of water and the bunker 13 cwt of coal. In full working order it weighed 23 tons 11 cwt.

In 1905, when the MNR went out of existence its engines became the property of the IoMR. In time *Thornhill* was allocated the running number 14 and *Caledonia* 15 by their new owners, and while on paper *Ramsey* and *Northern* were allotted nos 16 and 17 the numerals were never actually applied. In fact the latter two did relatively little work for the IoMR before being scrapped in 1923 and 1912 respectively.

Meanwhile, during the years 1894 to 1905, Beyer Peacock had supplied four more 2-4-0Ts to the IoMR, nos 8 to 11, the last two having been manufactured with slightly larger 3ft 3in diameter boilers. These additional purchases meant that at the end of 1905 the locomotive stock of the IoMR totalled 15.

In 1908 the fleet was augmented by the arrival of a further Beyer Peacock 2-4-0T no.12, then in 1910 by no.13 (these two being similar to nos 10 and 11), and finally in 1926 by no.16. The latter, named *Mannin*, and the only one fitted from new with a square-shaped cab, was the most powerful of the Beyer Peacock-built locomotives, having larger dimensions than its predecessors, including a 3ft 6in diameter boiler and 12in x 18in cylinders. Normally, *Mannin* was diagrammed to the more difficult Douglas to Port Erin route.

No further motive power was shipped to the island until 1961 when two 41-seater railcars, nos 19 and 20, were obtained at auction from the County Donegal Railways Joint Committee in Ireland following the closure of their lines. They had originally been put together in 1950/51 utilising power bogies supplied by Walker Bros (Wigan) Ltd, Gardner six-cylinder engines, with the bodywork constructed in the Great Northern Railway of Ireland Dundalk Works. They were the only diesels ever to travel over the 'northern lines' out of Douglas.

As regards liveries the MNR painted its locomotives in Tuscan red with black and vermilion lining, the IoMR having adopted a shade of dark green, the colours of the lining varying over the years. After 1905, perhaps surprisingly, it was to be some years before *Thornhill* and *Caledonia* appeared in IoMR colours, while the two Sharp Stewart engines never did receive a repaint. From 1945 Indian red with black and yellow lining became the standard, and then in 1967 Lord Ailsa decided the engines should sport apple green with the lining in white and black.

The accompanying table gives the present whereabouts or disposal details of the locomotives. For convenience, apart from the Sharp Stewart engines, they are listed in IoMR running number order. Also included are the three diesel locomotives purchased in more recent years, albeit that these have only operated over the short section of the Ramsey line that is still in use around Douglas station.

1. Official works photograph of Manx Northern Railway 2-4-0T no.2 constructed by Sharp Stewart of Manchester in 1879. Note the cast number plate below the builder's identification plate on the side of the tank. The nameplates *Northern* were attached later, one on each side of the front boiler ring. In 1912 it became the first IoMR locomotive to be scrapped. (H.Stevenson Collection)

**DOUGLAS, ST. JOHN'S, RAMSEY, and PEEL.—Isle of Man.**

Sec. and Man., Thos. Stowell, Douglas.

June 1922

| No. | Builder & Works no. | Year | Name | Location/Disposal |
|---|---|---|---|---|
| 1(a) | SS2885 | 1879 | *Ramsey* | Scrapped 1923 |
| 2(a) | SS2886 | 1879 | *Northern* | Scrapped 1912 |
| 1 | BP1253 | 1873 | *Sutherland* | IoMR |
| 2 | BP1254 | 1873 | *Derby* | Dismantled 1951 |
| 3 | BP1255 | 1873 | *Pender* | Sectioned exhibit Museum of Science & Industry, Manchester |
| 4 | BP1416 | 1874 | *Loch* | IoMR |
| 5 | BP1417 | 1874 | *Mona* | IoMR(b) |
| 6 | BP1524 | 1875 | *Peveril* | Port Erin Railway Museum |
| 7 | BP2038 | 1880 | *Tynwald* | Dismantled 1945 - frames etc exhibit at Port St Mary goods yard(b) |
| 8 | BP3610 | 1894 | *Fenella* | IoMR(b) |
| 9 | BP3815 | 1896 | *Douglas* | IoMR(b) |
| 10 | BP4662 | 1905 | *G.H.Wood* | IoMR |
| 11 | BP4663 | 1905 | *Maitland* | IoMR |
| 12 | BP5126 | 1908 | *Hutchinson* | IoMR |
| 13 | BP5382 | 1910 | *Kissack* | IoMR |
| 14(a) | BP2028 | 1880 | *Thornhill* | Privately preserved, near Ramsey |
| 15(a) | D2178 | 1885 | *Caledonia* | IoMR |
| 16 | BP6296 | 1926 | *Mannin* | Port Erin Railway Museum |
| 17(c) | Sc2086 | 1958 | *Viking* | IoMR |
| 19(d) | WkB | 1950 | | IoMR |
| 20(d) | WkB | 1951 | | IoMR |
| (e) | MR22021 | 1959 | | IoMR |
| (f) | MR40s280 | 1966 | | IoMR |

Notes:

| | |
|---|---|
| (a) | Originally owned by Manx Northern Railway - to IoMR 1905 |
| (b) | Owned by the Isle of Man Railway & Tramway Preservation Society |
| (c) | ex-Dortmund, Germany 1992 |
| (d) | ex-County Donegal Railways Joint Committee, Ireland 1961 |
| (e) | ex-Miller Engineering & Construction Ltd, Sandiacre, Derbyshire 1987 |
| (f) | ex-Neil Clayton, Ripon, North Yorkshire 1996, previously National Coal Board |

Builders:

| | |
|---|---|
| BP | Beyer Peacock & Co Ltd, Gorton Foundry, Manchester |
| D | Dübs & Co, Glasgow |
| MR | Motor Rail Ltd, Simplex Works, Bedford |
| Sc | Christoph Schöttler Maschinenfabrik GmbH, Diepholz, Germany |
| SS | Sharp Stewart & Co Ltd, Atlas Works, Manchester |
| WkB | Walker Bros (Wigan) Ltd, Pagefield Ironworks, Wigan |

June 1960

DOUGLAS, ST. JOHN'S, RAMSEY and PEEL—Isle of Man

| Miles | Down | am | am. | p.m. | p.m | p.m | | | |
|---|---|---|---|---|---|---|---|---|---|
| | Douglas ......... dep | .. | .. | 11 50 | 3 25 | .. | .. | .. | .. |
| | Union Mills ............. | .. | .. | † | † | .. | .. | .. | .. |
| | Crosby............... | .. | .. | † | 3 39 | .. | .. | .. | .. |
| | St. John's ......... arr | .. | .. | 12 13 | 3 48 | .. | .. | .. | .. |
| — | St. John's ....... dep | .. | .. | 12 18 | 3 53 | .. | .. | .. | .. |
| | Kirk Michael ......... | 8 10 | .. | 12 39 | 4 14 | .. | .. | .. | .. |
| 18½ | Ballaugh ............. | 8 18 | .. | 12 47 | 4 23 | .. | .. | .. | .. |
| 20½ | Sulby Glen ......... | 8 24 | .. | 12 53 | 4 29 | .. | .. | .. | .. |
| | Sulby Bridge ......... | 8 27 | .. | 12 56 | † | .. | .. | .. | .. |
| 5 | Ramsey ........... arr | 8 36 | .. | 1 5 | 4 40 | .. | .. | .. | .. |
| — | St. John's ......... dep | .. | .. | .. | .. | 4 56 | .. | .. | .. |
| 11½ | Peel ............... arr | .. | .. | .. | .. | 5 5 | .. | .. | .. |

| Miles | Up | a.m | a.m. | a.m. | a.m. | a.m | p.m |
|---|---|---|---|---|---|---|---|
| | Pee. ...... dep | 7 25 | .. | 8 5 | .. | .. | .. |
| | St. John's ........ arr | 7 34 | .. | 8 14 | .. | .. | .. |
| | Ramsey ....... dep | 6 45 | 7 30 | .. | 10 0 | .. | 4 5 |
| ⅜ | Sulby Bridge ..... | 6 55 | 7 40 | .. | 10 10 | .. | 4 15 |
| 4¼ | Sulby Glen ....... | 6 58 | 7 43 | .. | 10 13 | .. | 4 18 |
| 6¾ | Ballaugh ......... | 7 4 | 7 49 | .. | 10 19 | .. | 4 24 |
| 13 | Kirk Michael ..... | 7 12 | 7 56 | .. | 10 27 | .. | 4 32 |
| 16½ | St. John's ...... arr | .. | .. | .. | 10 47 | .. | .. |
| — | St. John's ....... dep | 7 34 | .. | 8 16 | 10 52 | .. | .. |
| | Crosby........... | 7 47 | .. | 8 26 | 11 2 | .. | .. |
| | Union Mills ........ | 7 54 | .. | .. | .. | .. | .. |
| 11½ | Douglas ......... arr | 8 0 | .. | 8 40 | 11 15 | .. | .. |

‡ Calls at St. Germain's by request.　† Request stop.

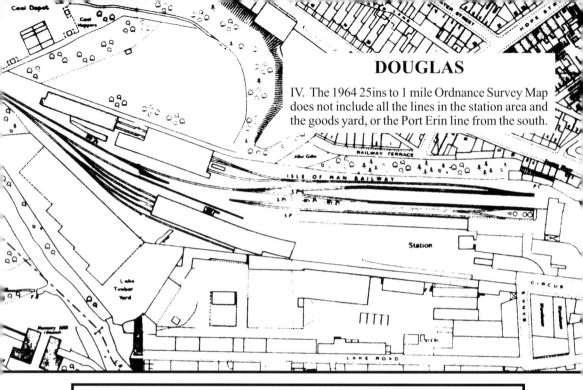

## DOUGLAS

IV. The 1964 25ins to 1 mile Ordnance Survey Map does not include all the lines in the station area and the goods yard, or the Port Erin line from the south.

| Receipts(a) | 1907 | 1917 | 1927 | 1937 | 1947 |
|---|---|---|---|---|---|
| Coaching(b) | £19,545 | £12,096 | £23,793 | £22,979 | £50,082(c) |
| Goods | £1,871 | £3,407 | £3,698 | £4,588 | £6,622 |

(a) Also includes income for Port Erin and Peel routes.
(b) All coaching stock receipts are for passengers and parcels, breakdown only available for 1947.
(c) Passenger £44,863, Parcels £5,219.

2.    These substantial Ruabon red brick buildings, completed by 1891, superseded the original wooden structures. They were observed from near the head of the harbour on 19th March 1967. The road on the left led to the goods yard. The main entrance doors remain in use today, while the block in the centre of the picture, once the main offices and refreshment rooms, now houses the Manx Government Customs and Excise Department. (D.J.Mitchell)

3.   Inside the booking hall intending second/third class passengers for the Peel and Ramsey line stations queued separately from those travelling first class, their tickets being issued from the Port Erin line window. The relevant signs by the hatches were still in place on 7th May 1997, almost 29 years after the last trains had departed for Peel and Ramsey, although the Peel and Ramsey board has since been removed to the Port Erin Railway Museum. Note, too, the large map of the island, depicting the Isle of Man Railway System and Omnibus Routes (the IoMR also operated bus services from 1928 trading as the Isle of Man Road Services), together with the large advert extolling the delights of the Manx Electric and Snaefell Mountain railways. Since 1991 much of the hall has been given over to a cafeteria with a mezzanine floor, the various models and other railway artefacts and memorabilia on display also contributing to the ambience. (T.Heavyside)

4.   This picture dates from soon after the turn of the century, as passengers off an incoming train at platform 5 make their way towards the exit. To the left is the imposing clock tower above the entrance by the junction of Bank Hill and Peel Road. The island platform normally used by the Peel and Ramsey services, on the north side of the station, is hidden by the coaching stock.
(Lens of Sutton Collection)

5.	Although the railway was closed at the time, some business was still being conducted at the goods yard in April 1966. A line of M wagons occupy the 'sunken siding' on the left. Beyond, near the neck of the yard, is the 320ft-long corrugated iron carriage shed of 1893 vintage and the signal box, while nearer the camera 1946-registered IoMR Morris Commercial lorry no.21 awaits its next assignment by a covered G van. (D.J.Mitchell)

6.	Canopies were erected over the platforms back in 1909. Flanking the engine release road are no.5 *Mona* at platform 3 and the ex-County Donegal railcars at platform 5 in July 1967. (D.J.Mitchell)

7. This signalman's view is of *Mona* leaving platforms 1 and 2 with the 10.20am service to Peel on 14th June 1968. By making use of the coaling and watering facilities at the side of the engine release road, opposite platform 4, engines could be serviced between duties without the need to return to the shed. The platform canopies were taken down ten years later in 1978. (G.D.King)

8. No.13 *Kissack* comes off shed as no.4 *Loch* bides time outside the workshops on 19th August 1971. Partly visible behind *Loch* is the body of former Cleminson coach no.N41, built in 1879 by the Swansea Wagon Co for the Manx Northern Railway. It did duty as the enginemens mess hut from 1964 until 1999. (T.Heavyside)

9.   Ten minutes later *Kissack* passes the signal box on its way out of Douglas with the 2.15pm to Port Erin. The signal box remained in use until 1982 when a major reordering of the station took place, the south side of the layout (including the goods yard) being taken out of commission and re-laid for car and bus parking purposes. At the same time colour-light signals, operated from the station offices, replaced the semaphores, while the footplate crews then had to move the points themselves by means of local ground levers. (T.Heavyside)

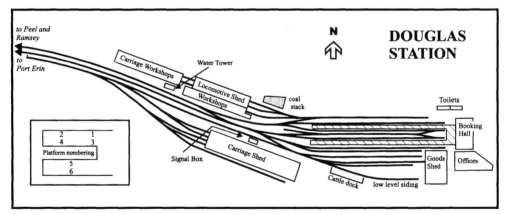

**DOUGLAS STATION**

to Peel and Ramsey

to Port Erin

Carriage Workshops

Water Tower

Locomotive Shed Workshops

coal stack

Toilets

Booking Hall

| | |
|---|---|
| 2 | 1 |
| 4 | 3 |
| Platform numbering | |
| 5 | |
| 6 | |

Signal Box

Carriage Shed

Cattle dock   low level siding

Goods Shed

Offices

V.  Track plan of the site as fully developed. Ramsey line services normally used platforms 1 to 4.

10.   Outside the shed by the coaling stage on 7th May 1997, long-serving driver John Elkin gives no.10 *G.H.Wood* a final polish in readiness for the day's work ahead. The Beyer Peacock builder's plate dated 1905 is affixed to the side of the cab. (T.Heavyside)

**Other views of Douglas station and its surrounds can be seen in our *Douglas to Port Erin* and *Douglas to Peel* albums.**

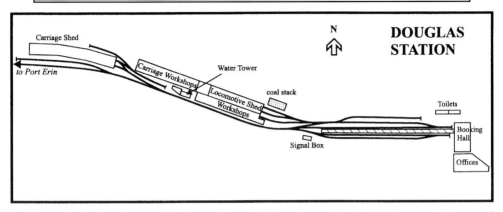

VI. The revised plan shows only the northern platform in use. Note that the space between the locomotive shed and carriage workshop has been roofed over.

11. A portrait taken in the shed yard shows 0-6-0T *Caledonia*, the only locomotive built for the Manx Northern Railway to work on the IoMR in recent times, as the driver shovels coal onto the footplate on 22nd August 1998. The engine is resplendent as MNR no.4 in a Tuscan red paint scheme. The Dübs diamond-shaped identification plate is attached to the cab side sheet. The engine currently sports a blue livery. (T.Heavyside)

12.   In the lined-out Indian red livery recently reintroduced as standard for the Beyer Peacock 2-4-0Ts, no.11 *Maitland* prepares to leave the former platforms 3 and 4 with the 2.0pm to Port Erin on 26th April 2001. The three coaches have been repainted in the 'new' corporate colours of red and cream (similar to that worn in earlier years) which has gradually replaced the previous dark purple lake, as seen on coach no.F32 on the left. The latter, a vestibule open third with 32 seats, was obtained from MRCW in 1905.  Visible above the leading carriage behind *Maitland* is the clock tower over the Peel Road entrance. This was restored in 1990. The former platforms 5 and 6 once occupied the area to the right of the fence. (T.Heavyside)

13.   In total 48 three-plank H series wagons were constructed for use on the island, the first, no.H1, by the Metropolitan Railway Carriage & Wagon Co in 1873. All had been scrapped by the early 1970s. Following the restoration of two-plank wagon no.M78 a couple of years earlier, the Isle of Man Steam Railway Supporters Association Mainland Area Group completed a replica of no.H1 in 2000. It was built in the workshops of the West Lancashire Light Railway at Hesketh Bank. During October 2003 the two wagons, with no.H1 on the right, are seen resting in the siding laid on the north side of the station in 1999. (T.Heavyside)

14.   Having stood isolated from the running lines since the station alterations of 1982, the signal box was moved to a position overlooking the exit from the platforms in 1999. The inside of the 36-lever box, manufactured by Dutton & Co Ltd of Worcester in 1892, was recorded on 23rd October 2003 as no.10 *G.H.Wood* shunted outside. None of the levers are presently connected to the points or signals. (T.Heavyside)

15.   On the same day, no.8 *Fenella* was observed from the top of the flight of steps leading to the signal box as it left with the 2.15pm service to Castletown. In recent years locomotives have been despatched to the mainland for major overhauls, *Fenella* having returned from England earlier in the year. Previous to this the engine had not been steamed since 1969. (T.Heavyside)

# QUARTER BRIDGE

16. Railcars nos 19 and 20 head back to Douglas during the Summer of 1967. A halt was opened here in May 1928. It was closed one year later. Today, a gate by the A1 Douglas to Peel road, on the other side of the cottage seen here in the right background, provides access to the start of the Steam Heritage Trail - see *Douglas to Peel* picture 30. (D.J.Mitchell)

# BRADDAN

17.   The station, first used in 1897, was unusual in that it was only available to passengers on Summer Sunday mornings in connection with the open-air services held at the nearby Kirk Braddan parish church. On this occasion, in July 1967, no.12 *Hutchinson* arrives from Douglas in good time for the service. The ticket office on the left was moved to Colby on the 'south line' in 1988 - see *Douglas to Port Erin* picture 97. (D.J.Mitchell)

# UNION MILLS

| Receipts | 1907 | 1917 | 1927 | 1937 | 1947 |
|---|---|---|---|---|---|
| Coaching | £327 | £342 | £451 | £283 | £359(a) |
| Goods | £33 | £68 | £148 | £16 | £6 |
| (a) Passenger £341, Parcels £18. | | | | | |

18.  One-time this was regarded as one of the most attractive stopping places on the line, the station and its surrounds being maintained in immaculate condition by the station master. The station officially closed in November 1954 although trains continued to call the following Summer. It was reopened by Lord Ailsa in 1967, and on a sunny afternoon in July of that year no.12 *Hutchinson* passes along the down loop, completed during 1906-07 along with the raised platform, with a train destined for Peel. The 1873 alignment is on the left. (D.J.Mitchell)

19.   No.15 *Caledonia* follows the original track through the station with an Isle of Man Steam Railway Supporters Association excursion to St John's on 2nd June 1968. This proved to be *Caledonia's* last assignment before it was restored to service in 1994. The leading coach, 'pairs' no.F75, formed in 1926 from the bodies off four-wheeled coaches nos A12 and C9, can be examined in the Port Erin Railway Museum. The siding leading off on the right was installed in 1907. (D.J.Mitchell)

20.   When the rails were removed and the rest of the site cleared in the mid-1970s the platform was left in position. Later, in 1990, this eight-ton hand crane with a 14ft-radius jib, obtained from Richard C.Gibbins & Co of Birmingham in 1893, was placed near the west end of the platform on a short piece of track. In the past it had formed part of the breakdown train. The photograph was taken on 27th April 2001. The opposite side of the crane can be studied in *Douglas to Peel* picture 43. (T.Heavyside)

# CROSBY

| Receipts | 1907 | 1917 | 1927 | 1937 | 1947 |
|----------|------|------|------|------|------|
| Coaching | £476 | £560 | £464 | £276 | £665(a) |
| Goods | £46 | £147 | £144 | £87 | £39 |
| (a) Passenger £631, Parcels £34. | | | | | |

21.   No.8 *Fenella* prepares to halt while in charge of the 3.25pm Douglas to Peel and Ramsey service on 12th June 1958. The corrugated iron goods shed, demolished in 1960, can be seen to the left of *Fenella*, with the cattle dock on the extreme left. The main station building is almost hidden by the locomotive, while the top of the west gable of the crossing-keepers lodge, on the far side of the level crossing, is visible on the right. (R.E.Gee)

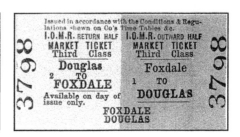

22. The front of the main building is seen on 18th March 1967. A close examination of the structure reveals a number of fine details. The level crossing over the B35 Crosby to St Mark's road is just off the picture to the right. Nothing now remains at this site except the stone-built crossing-keepers lodge which serves as a resting place for hikers intent on completing the Steam Heritage Trail. (D.J.Mitchell)

# ST JOHN'S

23. Ramsey trains used the tracks on the north side of the station. On 24th June 1926, with various railway personnel in attendance, no.10 *G.H.Wood* reposes by the outer face of the island platform. In the distance a cattle wagon is positioned in front of the carriage shed. The footbridge on which the photographer is standing was later declared unsafe and had to be taken down in 1945. (K.Nunn Collection/Locomotive Club of Great Britain)

| Receipts(a) | 1907 | 1917 | 1927 | 1937 | 1947 |
|---|---|---|---|---|---|
| Coaching | £1,007 | £1,010 | £1,198 | £775 | £1,560(b) |
| Goods | £139 | £163 | £679 | £263 | £168 |
| (a) Also includes income for Peel line. | | | | | |
| (b) Passenger £1,478, Parcels £82. | | | | | |

VII. Track plan of St John's and its approaches at its optimum. Initially, Manx Northern Railway trains from Ramsey terminated on the west side of the main highway, along what eventually became the turntable road.

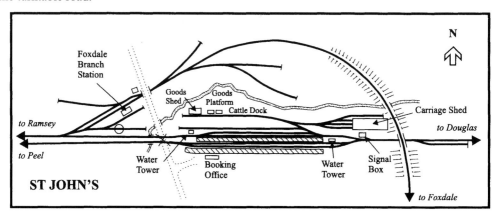

24.   A study of the east end of the layout on 8th April 1950. Flanked by the up starting signals, no.1 *Sutherland* occupies the Ramsey line by the water tower. The Peel lines are on the left with the junction points for the two routes just off the picture to the right. The wooden signal box, resting on a stone base, was erected at the expense of the Manx Northern Railway but was always manned by the IoMR. The box housed a ten-lever frame by Stevens & Son of London and Glasgow. On the right is the carriage shed. (J.D.Darby)

25.   The junction between the MNR and the Foxdale Railway was located some 250 yards or so to the west of the main station. In this view facing east, again on 8th April 1950, the former FR station building can be seen to the left of the semaphore signal in the foreground, by the road overbridge. The line to Peel is on the right. (J.D.Darby)

26.   Recorded on the same day as the previous two pictures, this 35ft-diameter turntable, capable of accepting loads of up to 55 tons, was the sole example on the IoMR. It was accessed from the Foxdale branch - the track leading to it can be discerned in the previous picture to the right of the signal post. The turntable had originally been ordered from Ransomes & Rapier Ltd of Ipswich by the West Clare Railway in Ireland, but as they were unable to accept delivery they sold it to the IoMR for £250-0s-0d in 1923. After the installation work was finished in March 1925, it was used from time to time to turn carriages around in an effort to equalise flange wear to the wheels and general weathering on each side. The table was removed in 1961 with the intention of relocating it where it would be more convenient for the operation of the recently-purchased single-ended ex-County Donegal railcars. In the event it remained stored at Douglas until it was eventually scrapped during the mid-1970s. (J.D.Darby)

27.   The 11.35am from Ramsey, consisting of two coaches and five freight wagons behind no.10 *G.H.Wood*, crosses the St John's to Castletown road at the approach to the station on 4th August 1951. A railway employee leans on the lever that operated the set of points that the train is about to negotiate. Behind him is a Stevens patent signal lever. A close-up of one of these levers can be examined in *Douglas to Port Erin* picture 74. When the MNR commenced services in 1879 these terminated on the land to the right of the train, any passengers for Douglas having to make their own way across the road to the IoMR station, although stock could be exchanged between the two railways by means of a crossover understood to have been installed near to where the junction for the Foxdale branch was eventually sited. In 1881 the MNR extended its track across the road by way of an independent level crossing into the IoMR station, with a new junction between the two systems provided at the east end (see picture 24), the original connection being removed. After this coaches from Ramsey could be attached to IoMR trains running through to Douglas. The track in use here was laid in 1886, the previous through line being shortened on either side of the roadway so as to form a couple of sidings. (J.D.Darby)

28.  The site of what a couple of years later became the Foxdale Railway station was first utilised by the MNR in 1884, when a wooden hut sufficed for station requirements. The FR building, located by the bridge, dates from 1886, the layout being controlled from the nine-lever ground frame on the right at the west end of the platform. The frame had three spare levers. After 1906 the building was used as a house by the St John's station master, while from 1927 the branch trains reversed in and out of the main station, rather than starting and ending their journeys here. When photographed on 29th June 1955 the running line towards Foxdale had almost disappeared under a mass of verdant vegetation. A rake of ex-MNR Cleminson coaches are stored on the loop line. (H.Ballantyne)

29.   On a number of occasions during the day the main station became rather busy as it dealt with the dividing and joining-up of trains from and to Douglas and the interchange of passengers between various services, relative peace descending on the area during the interim! On the same day as the previous picture passengers prepare to board the 2.15pm from Douglas to Ramsey with no.5 *Mona* in charge, while others walk towards the carriages of a service heading in the opposite direction. To the right of the photographer a Peel train was also awaiting the 'right away' signal. (H.Ballantyne)

30.   Later the same afternoon no.1 *Sutherland* draws forward with the Ramsey portion of the 3.25pm from Douglas. The carriages had been detached from the section bound for Peel by the hoardings on the right. The bridge in the background, built wide enough to accommodate double track in case of need, supported the Foxdale branch. (H.Ballantyne)

31.   The last major development was the construction of a 288ft-long, three-road corrugated iron carriage shed in 1905. Outside the shed on 1st August 1962 is 'pairs' 60-seater third class vehicle no.F58. The IoMR created 26 such 'pairs', the first in 1909 and the final one in 1926, by mounting the bodies of two former four-wheeled coaches on a new bogie underframe. No.F58 was formed in 1922 from the bodies of nos B18 and C3, both constructed by the Metropolitan Railway Carriage & Wagon Co in 1873/74, on a chassis obtained from the same source. The strip hiding the gap between the two bodies, fitted during the 1930s, is clearly evident, as is the double footboard, a necessary addition to assist passengers since many of the stations had no raised platform. No.F58 was dismantled in 1967, the frame seeing further use for a short time as a container carrier between Castletown and Douglas (see *Douglas to Port Erin* pictures 63 and 80). (J.L.Stevenson)

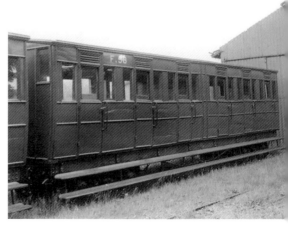

32.   For its passenger services the MNR decided on a series of 14 30ft-long six-wheeled coaches from the Swansea Wagon Co. The wheel arrangement was to a design patented by James Cleminson of London whereby each axle was carried in its own frame, the centre one being able to slide laterally from side to side while the two at the outer ends, which had linkages to the centre frame, were pivoted centrally. By this means each individual wheel-set remained more or less fully aligned with the track at all times and thus, even when travelling round curves, there was very little side pressure on the rails with a consequent marked reduction in flange and rail wear. Moreover, they were cheaper to build than coaches with conventional bogies, while passengers benefitted from a much smoother ride compared to a four-wheeled vehicle. The assembly was ideally suited to railways where some tight radius curves had to be negotiated and was popular with a number of narrow gauge concerns. For a more detailed description and drawings of the Cleminson principle see our *Branch Line to Southwold* album. The MNR Cleminson coaches were all delivered in 1879 and numbered 1 to 14. The first two, designated as first class, had 42 seats. The rest, two composites (nos 3 and 4) and ten third class, could each carry up to 60 people. After the merger with the IoMR twelve were renumbered F40 to F51 and subsequently as nos N40 to N51. Two, MNR nos 8 and 12, never received IoMR running numbers, being withdrawn in 1905 and 1904 respectively. However, during their IoMR days the Cleminsons saw comparatively little use, spending much of their time in storage at St John's. Third class example, MNR no.9 latterly no.N47 and looking rather shabby, was stabled near the carriage shed during the Summer of 1966. Its original no.9 numerals can just about be deciphered on the faded paintwork near the roofline at each end, while some of the underframe linkages can be seen above the lower footboard. The coach was destroyed by the fire which engulfed the shed in December 1975. Today, one of the Cleminsons, composite MNR no.3, later no.N42, now owned by the Isle of Man Railway & Tramway Preservation Society, remains in store at Douglas. Further, MNR nos 1, 6 and 14 (IoMR nos N40, N45 and N51) have also survived in private ownership, no.6 on the island and the other two in England. (D.J.Mitchell)

33.　In July 1967, with the Peel lines in the foreground, no.11 *Maitland* runs in from the east with a train for Ramsey. The leading coach is bogie brake third no.F48 built by MRCW in 1923. The next vehicle is a bogie guard composite constructed by Hurst Nelson of Motherwell in 1899 as MNR no.16, and renumbered F37 by the IoMR. The latter was moved to England in 1974 while no.F48 is still available for service. Propped against the nearside signal post is the bicycle used to reach the signal box by the well-regarded Station Master George Crellin. On this occasion he has already returned the Ramsey line semaphore to the horizontal position (the lower of the two signal arms on the far right of the picture) following the movement of the train across the junction. Shortly, no doubt, he will be hurrying along in order to supervise the departure of the train for the north. (D.J.Mitchell)

⟶

34.　Almost hidden by foliage when viewed from the road overbridge on 27th April 2001, the former Foxdale Railway station building survives as a dwelling-house. The decorative yellow quoins used in its construction stand out. As for the old platform, this was completely camouflaged by vegetation with one or two hens happily pecking amongst the grass. There is very little else to remind visitors that this was once an important railway junction, especially since the redevelopment of much of the site (this was cleared back in 1976) for the new St John's Primary School, opened in January 2003. That is apart from a sign marking the Steam Heritage Trail pathway to Quarter Bridge. (T.Heavyside)

**Other views of the route between Douglas and St.Johns are numbered 23-85 in the *Douglas to Peel* volume album.**

# SOUTH OF ST JOHN'S

35.   This late 1930s view is from the Foxdale branch train as it passes the sand and gravel pit sidings shortly after threading beneath the Castletown road at St John's. A ventilated G van is at the rear of the train. (R.Shepherd)

| ST. JOHN'S and FOXDALE.—Isle of Man. | | | | | | | | | | | | | | |
|---|---|---|---|---|---|---|---|---|---|---|---|---|---|---|
| | **Up.** | **Week Days only.** | | | | | | **Down.** | **Week Days only.** | | | | | |
| Miles. | | mrn | aft | | | | Miles. | | mrn | aft | | | | |
| | St. John's..........dep. | 9 45 | 2 45 | | | | | Foxdale..............dep. | 1620 | 3 10 | | | | |
| 1¼ | Waterfall.............. | c | c | | | | 1 | Waterfall.............. | c | c | | | | |
| 2¼ | Foxdale............arr. | 9 59 | 2 59 | | | | 2¼ | St. John's *(above)*...arr. | 1634 | 3 24 | | | | |
| | | | | c Stops when required. | | | | | | | | | | |

June 1922

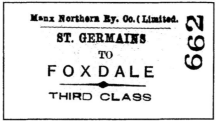

Manx Northern Ry. Co.( Limited.
**ST. GERMAINS**
TO
**FOXDALE**
THIRD CLASS
662

36. With Greeba Mountain (on the right) and Slieau Ruy, standing respectively 1,383ft and 1,570ft above sea level, overlooking proceedings, no.6 *Peveril* climbs the severe gradient away from St John's towards Foxdale on 4th July 1933. This particular coach, equipped with a better braking system than the MNR Cleminsons, was specially constructed for use on the branch by the Oldbury Carriage & Wagon Co in 1886. Originally MNR no.17, it was renumbered 15 in 1899 and after acquisition by the IoMR F39. In 1968, after standing out of use for many years, it was refurbished by Lord Ailsa as a camping coach for his own use and parked in Douglas goods yard (see *Douglas to Peel* picture 12). Commonly referred to as 'The Foxdale Coach', it was restored to working order for the MNR centenary celebrations in 1979. (H.C.Casserley)

37. Within 15 seconds or so, the train seen in the previous picture would have passed over the Douglas to St John's line by this bridge. Here we see no.1 *Sutherland* en route to Foxdale with a rake of five empty M wagons on 30th May 1939. The St John's signal box and the down home signals can be seen beyond the bridge, while the siding in the foreground, to the left of the main line, served a sand and gravel pit. (W.A.Camwell/Stephenson Locomotive Society)

# WATERFALL

38.   This stopping place served the village of Lower Foxdale, which at one-time before opening was to have been titled as such, the name Hamilton Waterfall (a nearby local feature) also being proposed. In the event plain Waterfall sufficed, although on occasions it was referred to as Waterfalls, and tickets were printed with the plural version. Initially, there was a passing loop with movements governed from a Stevens ground frame, but by the late 1890s the loop had been lifted and the frame taken out of commission. The station was then unmanned. The wooden hut, erected about 1905, replaced a timber structure brought from St John's when the railway opened. The station became a 'request stop' in 1928. Here we are looking towards St John's on a sunny 3rd July 1933. (H.C.Casserley)

## SOUTH OF WATERFALL

39.   This is a 1966 panorama looking north. The Castletown to Ramsey road is behind the embankment on the left which, just a little way to the north, dived under the railway at Luke's bridge by means of a rather dangerous double-bend. The bridge has since been demolished and the bends eased. Slieau Whallian, its peak rising 1,094ft above sea level, provides the backcloth. (A.M.Davies)

# FOXDALE

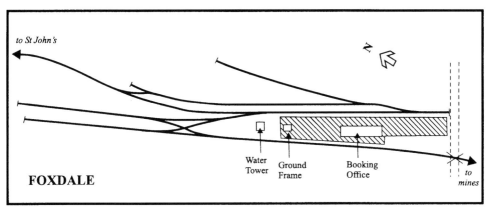

VIII.  Track Plan of Foxdale.

| Receipts | **1907** | **1917** | **1927** | **1937** | **1947** |
|----------|----------|----------|----------|----------|----------|
| Coaching | £122 | £76 | £181 | £113 | £62(a) |
| Goods | £964 | £165 | £36 | £2278 | Nil |
| (a) Passenger £59, Parcels £3. | | | | | |
| Note: Although after 1940 there were no scheduled passenger trains, for a number of years the annual station returns were still completed, presumably in respect of the income from the bus service. | | | | | |

40.    The celebratory opening of the branch, including some appropriate music by the Foxdale Brass Band, took place on 16th August 1886 when a number of railway officials, along with a few guests, clustered on the platform by no.4 *Caledonia*. The coach is Cleminson composite MNR no.3 (later IoMR no.N42). The up starting signal can be seen to the right of the station building. (Manx National Heritage)

# Isle of Man Railway Company

# PARTIAL CLOSING
## OF
# FOXDALE RAILWAY STATION

The Isle of Man Railway Company hereby give NOTICE that on and after Monday, the 3rd June, 1912, the Foxdale Railway Station will be CLOSED until further notice for the Booking of Passengers, Parcels, and Goods, EXCEPT DURING THE TIMES BETWEEN THE ARRIVAL AND DEPARTURE OF EACH TRAIN, which times are duly advertised in the Company's Time Tables.

All persons expecting Goods or Parcels must have them taken away during the times the Station is open, unless arranged otherwise with the Officials of the Company.

THOS. STOWELL, Secretary and Manager.

Douglas, 27th May, 1912.

Printed at "Herald" Office, Douglas.

41.   No.6 *Peveril* is ready to leave with the 5.30pm to St John's on 3rd July 1933. The station building, constructed of red brick with yellow quoins, had been unmanned since June 1912 (it was converted into a house during the mid-1920s), with all business having to be transacted between the arrival and departure of passenger trains. The clock tower, pointing skyward above the carriage, was built in 1901 *for the benefit of Foxdale* by the Isle of Man Mining Co Ltd. It continues to serve the local community. (H.C.Casserley)

42.   The next three illustrations date from the late 1930s. Here, at the back of the station, we are looking down the steeply-inclined track that connected the branch with the former lead mining area. The route to St John's curves round the spoil heap on the right. Empty wagons destined for the mines had to be reversed twice, once by the station platform (out of sight on the right), and then again in one of the two sidings beyond the scissors crossover. By this time the semaphore signals erected at the start of services, and the Stevens nine-lever ground frame positioned at the north end of the platform, had been abandoned. The points were then moved by local levers. The brick building on the right is the water tower. (R.Shepherd)

43.  We now set our sights in the other direction towards the mines complex. In the foreground is the A24 Foxdale to Douglas road. In 2001 a short section of track was visible in the roadway, although this has since been covered over. (R.Shepherd)

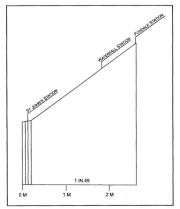

IX.  Gradient Profile St John's to Foxdale.

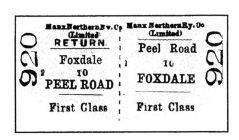

44.    Having walked into the abandoned mining area, the photographer turned to record this industrial landscape looking back towards St John's. The south elevation of the station is evident on the extreme right. (R.Shepherd)

45.  No.1 *Sutherland* slowly runs towards the buffer stops with five M wagons on 29th May 1939. At the end of the platform is the brick water tower, complete with yellow quoins in a similar style to the main building, with a cylindrical tank on top. (W.A.Camwell/Stephenson Locomotive Society)

46.   The station area is seen looking towards the south on 3rd July 1955, some 15 years after the last regular passenger train had plodded up the branch. The main building was then occupied by a local quarrying company. The entrance gate is on the left by the road. (S.C.Nash)

47.   Photographed from almost the same standpoint as picture 45 this was the scene over sixty years later on 25th April 2001. Nowadays, there is hardly anything to indicate that there was ever a railway here, the ugly spoil heaps also having been removed. In recent times the building, with the front recess suitably enclosed, has been put to good use as a community centre, while the grounds of the 1991-built Foxdale Primary School extend across the old boundary line of the railway on the right-hand side. (T.Heavyside)

# WEST OF ST JOHN'S

48.   We now return to St John's in order to resume our journey towards Ramsey. Running parallel with the line from Peel, having just passed the St John's home signal, no.1 *Sutherland* coasts towards the station with the 1.50pm from Ramsey on 30th June 1955. At St John's the two carriages were attached to the coaches forming the 2.30pm from Peel for the remainder of the journey to Douglas. (R.E.Gee)

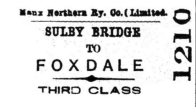

49.   The Ramsey line home signal was photographed on 18th March 1967. The signal arm was lowered to the 'off' position by means of a Stevens patent lever positioned at the west end of the station by the level crossing (see picture 27). The opposite side of the signal is featured in *Douglas to Peel* picture 87. (D.J.Mitchell)

50.   Just to the east of the two independent 30ft-span wrought iron bridges by which the Ramsey and Peel routes crossed over the River Neb, the sad sight of some of the lifted rails from the Peel line being dragged towards St John's was witnessed in September 1974. The Ramsey rails on the left, much overgrown after six years of inactivity, were awaiting a similar fate. (D.J.Mitchell)

51.   In far happier times a few years earlier on 5th June 1968, no.10 *G.H.Wood* strides over the River Neb with a Douglas to Ramsey service. A train for Peel can be observed in the distance and it too will shortly cross the river, but at a slightly lower level, by the bridge on the right. (D.J.Mitchell)

52. Shortly after passing over the Neb the line changed from a westerly to a more northerly direction. Here no.11 *Maitland* draws its three carriages over the A1 Douglas to Peel road at Ballaleece and climbs towards Peel Road with a train for Ramsey in July 1967. The course of the Peel route runs alongside the fence to the right of *Maitland's* chimney. In the background is the northern edge of the Southern Upland Massif. (D.J.Mitchell)

# PEEL ROAD

53.   The station, known as Poortown for the first two years of its existence, opened in June 1883. It was the nearest Manx Northern Railway station to Peel, although to reach the station from the fishing port entailed a walk of over one mile along what later became the A20 road. The station was unstaffed after 1937. With the guard peering out from the rear carriage, the station facilities, including a raised platform, along with the entrance path behind the large nameboard on the right, were observed from a departing Ramsey-bound train on 19th April 1950. (H.C.Casserley)

| Receipts | 1907 | 1917 | 1927 | 1937 | 1947 |
|----------|------|------|------|------|------|
| Coaching | £255 | £266 | £215 | £13 | £29(a) |
| Goods | £9 | £10 | £948 | £132 | £43 |
| (a) Passenger £27, Parcels £2. | | | | | |

54.    The station was closed in June 1952.  By August 1961, when this photograph was taken looking towards Ramsey, the wooden-sided, corrugated tin-roofed station building was looking rather forlorn, with even a Bovril advertising board propped incongruously against the side wall. In the shadow of the trees by the bridge is the body of a four-wheeled passenger brake van - believed to be no.E6 built by the Metropolitan Railway Carriage & Wagon Co for the IoMR in 1876. It was placed here in 1911 and for a time acted as a goods shed, but in the main simply served as a store for the permanent way gang. (H.Stevenson)

55. No.11 *Maitland* storms past while heading for Ramsey in July 1967. (D.J.Mitchell)

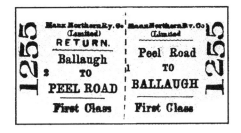

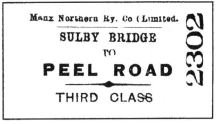

# NORTH OF PEEL ROAD

56.   Immediately beyond the station, there was a short siding and loading bank on the east side of the line from 1885 until 1948. It was served by a 2ft 0in gauge horse-drawn tramway from the nearby Poortown Quarry, which supplied aggregate for the Highways Board. This was the scene looking north from the A20 road overbridge on 28th June 1974, with the old loading platform on the right, by this time almost completely hidden. The main running line had also almost disappeared under the vegetation after nearly six years of disuse. (J.L.Stevenson)

# SOUTH OF ST GERMAIN'S

57.   Amidst some idyllic countryside no.14 *Thornhill* scurries cab-first towards St John's with the 8.50am mixed train from Ramsey on 8th July 1955. The leading coach no.F42 is a brake third obtained by the IoMR from the Metropolitan Railway Carriage & Wagon Co in 1907, while at the rear are four M wagons. In the distance, the level crossing gates by St Germain's station have already been reopened to traffic travelling along what was then the A3 Peel to Ramsey road - since reclassified as the A4 between Peel and Kirk Michael. (Lens of Sutton Collection)

58.   In July 1967, for this panorama of the same stretch of line seen in the previous picture, the photographer chose a higher vantage point a little further inland. The course of the railway can be followed just above the trees as railcars nos 20 and 19 approach the station. Beyond the farm buildings is the Irish Sea. From this area, on a clear day, the Mourne Mountains in Ireland can be readily identified. (D.J.Mitchell)

# ST GERMAIN'S

59.  Initially, until Peel Road opened in June 1883, the station served the residents of Peel, despite the fact that the centre of the town was almost two miles away. Shortly after opening, a passing loop and a siding were installed. They were removed in the early 1890s, only for the loop to be reinstated in 1926. Three years later, a loading dock and an accompanying siding, seen here on the left-hand side of the photograph, were brought into use for the despatch of sand and gravel collected from the nearby shore at White Strand. Here, *Thornhill* is en route south on 8th July 1955 with the same train seen a couple of minutes later in picture 57. (S.C.Nash)

60.  Shortly after the station had officially closed in July 1961 a Beyer Peacock 2-4-0T passes with a northbound train. However, as in past years when the station did not appear in the timetable, it was not unknown for passengers to alight or board here. The former loop line and the siding had been lifted during the late 1950s. (D.Lawrence/H.Davies Collection)

61. No.10 *G.H.Wood* drifts by with a Ramsey to Douglas service on 3rd June 1968. This fine Peel red sandstone building had been used as a dwelling house since 1906. It was hardly complemented by the dilapidated corrugated iron shed that was used by the railway for its day to day requirements. (D.J.Mitchell)

| Receipts | 1907 | 1917 | 1927 | 1937 | 1947 |
|----------|------|------|------|------|------|
| Coaching | £18 | £18 | £46 | £83 | £190(a) |
| Goods | (b) | (c) | (d) | £2 | £52 |

(a) Passenger £172, Parcels £18.
(b) Actual 8s 1d (40p).
(c) Actual 4s 8d (23p).
(d) Actual 9s 9d (49p).

62. The station site is seen looking towards St John's on 18th May 2002. The building is now privately owned and amongst a number of improvements are the new windows on the first floor of the two gables. The old iron shed at the south end has been removed. (T.Heavyside)

# NORTH OF ST GERMAIN'S

63.   The 3½-mile length of the former trackbed along the spectacular section onwards to Glen Mooar is now a public footpath. It has also been incorporated into the Raad ny Foillan (Road of the Gull), a 95-mile long circular footpath around the Manx coast. This explanatory sign is positioned just to the right of the access gate seen in the previous picture. (T.Heavyside)

This Public Footpath follows part of the track of the old Steam Railway line from Douglas to Ramsey via St. Johns. This part of the line was opened in 1879 by the Manx Northern Railway Co. and was amalgamated with the Isle of Man Railway Co. Ltd. In 1905. The line finally closed in 1968 and the permanent way was removed in 1974. The land is now owned by the Government Property Trustees who have dedicated a Public Footpath from here to Glen Mooar. About 3½ MLS.

64.   A Beyer Peacock 2-4-0T drifts south away from 'The Donkey Bank' at Lynague with three coaches from Ramsey in July 1967. Along the coast, above the stone bridge which at one-time provided access to a sandpit, can be seen St Patrick's Isle, the site of Peel Castle and the ruins of the thirteenth century St German's cathedral, and to its left the town of Peel. In the background, rising above the narrow streets of Peel, is the 1806-built 50ft-high tower on Corrins Hill. (D.J.Mitchell)

65.   Looking in the opposite direction from the same vantage point used for the previous picture, the photographer observed no.11 *Maitland* after it had just passed the headland at Gob-y-Deigan (Devil's Mouth) with a Ramsey to Douglas service, again in July 1967. From 1887 until 1914 a halt was located in the area to the back of the train, with footpaths from the halt leading both to the main road (out of sight on the right) and down to the beach below. The permanent way hut once served as a shelter for anyone waiting for a train here. (D.J.Mitchell)

66.   No.14 *Thornhill* travels above the cliffs on the north side of the headland at Gob-y-Deigan while returning to Ramsey on 8th July 1955. The trackbed along this stretch tended to be a little unstable and over the years required constant monitoring and much remedial work. (S.C.Nash)

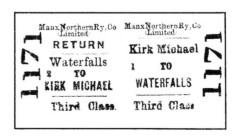

# GLEN MOOAR

67.   When first built the 180ft-long viaduct over the narrow glen consisted of three wrought iron lattice girders of equal length. Forty years later the spans had deteriorated somewhat and in 1921 were replaced by lattice steel girders. Riding 75ft above the bed of the river below, no.12 *Hutchinson* crosses the viaduct on its way to Douglas in July 1955. (Lens of Sutton Collection)

68.   No.11 *Maitland* heads north towards Ramsey in July 1967. From this viewpoint, looking towards the Irish Sea, it is readily apparent how much buffeting the structure must have withstood over the decades from the prevailing westerly winds. (D.J.Mitchell)

69.  On this occasion the viaduct is seen from the west looking inland, as no.10 *G.H.Wood* gingerly runs south with a couple of coaches in tow on 3rd June 1968. The path on the right leads up the glen to Spooyt Vane (White Spout) waterfall, one of the highest on the island. (D.J.Mitchell)

70.  The girders were removed in 1975 although, as seen from the south side of the glen in October 2003, the pillars and buttresses were left in place. Walkers who have traced the path from St Germain's who wish to continue further north along the route of the former railway, must first make a detour of a little under half-a-mile via the main road to the site of the former West Berk level crossing, just off the picture to the left of the cottage on the other side of the glen. (T.Heavyside)

# GLEN WYLLIN

71.   Initially the glen was bridged by three 65ft-long iron lattice girders supported by two stone piers. From the 1890s the glen, which covers almost 20 acres, was developed as a pleasure park, and being conveniently situated close to Kirk Michael station became a popular destination for a day's relaxation. In 1935 it was purchased by the IoMR, under whose auspices the facilities were enhanced even further. In its heyday visitors were able to enjoy bowls, tennis, boating, dancing and concerts etc, as well as a pleasant stroll down to the shore. Earlier, in 1915, the viaduct's three spans had had to be renewed, a plate girder construction being the preferred option. With many people taking advantage of a pleasant afternoon the appeal of the glen is evident, as a Beyer Peacock 2-4-0T rumbles overhead in the direction of Kirk Michael station during the 1920s. Unusually, the locomotive is running without a back cab sheet. (Lens of Sutton Collection)

Isle of Man Ry. Co., Limited.
PORT ERIN
TO
KIRK MICHAEL
FIRST CLASS.

086

72.   Only three day-trippers appear present, by the kiosk under the central span of the viaduct, as no.3 *Pender* passes some 55ft above the floor of the valley with the 11.35am Ramsey to Douglas service on 2nd June 1952. Behind the two passenger coaches are a number of unroofed livestock wagons. (J.D.Darby)

73.   During the 1950s and early 1960s the popularity of the glen gradually waned, while the Summer of 1967 proved to be the penultimate season when it was possible to look down on the valley from the lofty heights of the viaduct. In July of that year no.11 *Maitland* cautiously traverses the gorge and prepares to stop at Kirk Michael. The train is composed of four open vestibule coaches supplied by the Metropolitan Railway Carriage & Wagon Co in 1905. The leading vehicle is no.F31. (D.J.Mitchell)

74.  As at Glen Mooar, when the girders were dismantled in 1975 the masonry supports were left standing. Three years later, in 1978, after a short period in private ownership, the glen was purchased by the Government, and it is now one of seventeen Manx National Glens (as is Glen Mooar). A camp site was established during the early 1980s. This was the tranquil scene looking inland, with the rounded peak of Slieau Freoaghane 1,601ft above sea level dominant in the background, on 18th May 2002. (T.Heavyside)

# KIRK MICHAEL

75. No.14 *Thornhill* stops briefly while working to Douglas with a freight train consisting of a van and five cattle wagons on 10th April 1950. At the time the railway possessed 19 vans built by various manufacturers between 1873 and 1921, including some by the IoMR and the MNR themselves. As regards the cattle wagons, over the years, in total, 32 were on the books of the IoMR at one time or another, the majority having been put together in the company's own workshops, including some constructed during the early 1920s to replace older worn out examples. The vans were numbered with a G prefix and the cattle wagons a letter K. In the siding at the north end of the yard are a couple of M series two-plank wagons. (J.D.Darby)

| Receipts | 1907 | 1917 | 1927 | 1937 | 1947 |
|---|---|---|---|---|---|
| Coaching | £754 | £725 | £1,093 | £901 | £1,524(a) |
| Goods | £165 | £314 | £349 | £151 | £94 |
| (a) Passenger £1,384, Parcels £140. | | | | | |

76.   The red sandstone, slate-roofed station building was photographed on the sunny afternoon of 7th August 1950. Notice the large nameboard, the parcels trolley, a couple of milk churns awaiting collection, and the prominent enamel sign attached to the north gable advertising 'the smokers match' Swan Vestas. Electric lighting had been installed in 1936. (J.D.Darby)

77.   The 12.35pm from Ramsey to Douglas straddles the level crossing at the south end of the site, while no.1 *Sutherland* has its water tanks replenished on 28th June 1955. Trailing at the rear of the formation are three M wagons sandwiched between two G vans. The loop line had been extended over the crossing back in 1883. (H.Ballantyne)

78. A photo from 18th February 1958 shows trains passing. On this occasion, the locomotives changed trains so that the crews could return to their bases with their own engines. The stone wagons did not have continuous brakes. (A.G.W.Garraway)

79. This view looking towards the northern terminus on 22nd August 1961 has the level crossing gates in the foreground. The stone goods shed had replaced the original MNR building in 1923, the contractors being paid £408-12s-0d (£408-60). The station clock on the south gable continued to keep good time, while the advert for Swan Vestas remained in position on the other gable. There were also many adverts for Petter Oil Engines & Electric Lighting Plants around at the time, as seen on the south facing wall of the goods shed. (J.L.Stevenson)

80.   The water tank was positioned at the end of the single line section from St Germain's where it could be used by engines travelling in either direction. Here, no.10 *G.H.Wood* takes water while working the 10.20am Douglas to Ramsey service, before drawing forward into the station on 3rd June 1968. The points at the start of the loop line are clearly visible, as are the adjacent lever and connecting rod. Behind the fence on the left is the footpath leading from the station to Glen Wyllin. (D.J.Mitchell)

81.   The site is now utilised by the Isle of Man Fire Service - a fire engine prepared ready for its next call to duty can be seen inside the adapted goods shed on 18th May 2002. Appropriately, in recent years, a level crossing gate has hung at the side of the road, while a short section of track has been relaid. Remnants of the original loop line can be discerned in the carriageway. (T.Heavyside)

# KIRK MICHAEL STEAM CENTRE

82.   The centre, just a short walk away from the station, was established in the mid-1960s. In June 1968 the 2ft 0in gauge 2-4-0T *Sea Lion* (W.G.Bagnall works no.1484 of 1896) was obtained from the defunct Groudle Glen Railway on the east coast of the island. *Sea Lion* is seen looking rather the worse for wear, together with a traction-engine, in September 1968. The centre was closed in 1981 whereupon *Sea Lion* was transported to Loughborough. It was repatriated two years later and can often be seen at work on its original stamping ground on the 1983-reopened Groudle Glen Railway. (A.Matthewman/Breese Stamp Co)

Manx Northern Ry. Co.(Limited.

**SULBY BRIDGE**
TO
**UNION MILLS**

THIRD CLASS

353

# BISHOP'S COURT HALT

83.   From the middle years of the thirteenth century Bishopscourt (the house itself was variously spelt as one word or two), approximately one and a half miles north of Kirk Michael, was the palatial home of successive Bishops of Sodor and Man. Prior to the construction of the railway, a strip of land at the back of the grounds was acquired by the MNR from the ecclesiastical authorities, and an agreement made to provide a halt for the use of the Bishop, members of his staff and visitors. In later years, on a number of occasions, the IoMR endeavoured to restrict this arrangement and the halt fell into disuse after 1950. A simple bench seat marked the stopping place. Entry was gained by a flight of steps from the Bishop's private grounds. Standing proud on the skyline to the north in April 1950 is the gate-keepers cottage at Orrisdale no.1 crossing, from where the fish-tailed signal seen here was operated. Since 1974 the Bishop has lived in more modest accommodation, at first in Ramsey before moving to Douglas in 1977, enabling the diocese to sell Bishopscourt. (J.D.Darby)

84. At Orrisdale no.1 the railway crossed a minor road leading to the village of the same name. Trains were scheduled to call here in 1882 and 1883 and 'by request' for a short time afterwards. There was also a siding until the mid-1890s. Double gates protected the crossing with a pair of wicket-gates for the use of pedestrians on the south side. The signal by the lodge indicated whether or not the gates at Orrisdale no.2 crossing, a little further to the north, had been closed to road traffic. The negative of this print was exposed during September 1968. (A.Matthewman/Breese Stamp Co)

85. At Orrisdale no.2 crossing the wicket-gates were on the north side. When the crew of a southbound train sighted the signal opposite the lodge in the lowered 'off' position, they knew that the gates at Orrisdale no.1 had already been opened in their favour. This photograph was taken on 9th April 1950. (J.D.Darby)

# BALLAUGH

86. The signal governing the approach to the station from the south is seen on 9th April 1950. The station is beyond the level crossing gates, and nearer the camera is the wrought iron bridge which carried the railway over the Ballaugh river. (J.D.Darby)

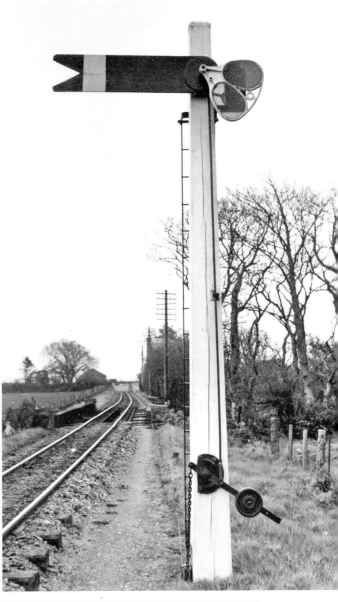

| Receipts | 1907 | 1917 | 1927 | 1937 | 1947 |
|---|---|---|---|---|---|
| Coaching | £643 | £699 | £1,000 | £471 | £1,110(a) |
| Goods | £91 | £141 | £219 | £76 | £124 |
| (a) Passenger £1,019, Parcels £91. | | | | | |

87.   Ten years later, on 13th April 1960, the red sandstone building is eyed from a departing Douglas to Ramsey train. No doubt many passengers would notice the well-maintained hedges and the palm tree. In the background, behind the village, are the foothills at the northern extremity of the Northern Upland Massif. (H.Stevenson)

→

88.   This is a pedestrian's view of the station looking towards Ramsey from the A10 road, which links Ballaugh with Ramsey via Jurby and Bride. The loop line was lengthened over the level crossing in 1883. Two M wagons stand on the goods loop created in 1923 from what had previously just been a siding, when a second connection was installed near the level crossing. Behind the wagons is the cattle bank. Part of the goods shed is visible to the left of the flagpole. The photograph is dated 22nd August 1961. (H.Stevenson)

→

89.   No.10 *G.H.Wood* makes a vigorous exit with a Douglas to Ramsey train on 3rd June 1968. The loading bank is on the right. By this time the trackbed had a somewhat neglected appearance. (D.J.Mitchell)

90.  This close-up of the stone-built goods shed is from 3rd August 1968. Attached to the side wall is yet more advertising material for Petter Oil Engines and Swan Vestas matches! (J.L.Stevenson)

91.  In 1979 the area was spruced up as a Manx Millennium project and designated Ballaugh Park. The goods shed was restored by Ballaugh cubs in 1995, although the main station building was not so fortunate, having already been demolished and a bungalow erected on the same plot. The park often proves a pleasant place to rest awhile and perhaps contemplate what has gone before, but this was far from the case on 19th May 2002 when the author endured a day of gale force winds and almost constant heavy rain! (T.Heavyside)

# WILD LIFE PARK

92.  For a number of years from 1882, during MNR days, on the St John's side of what was officially known as Ballavolley crossing, there was a siding which served a nearby stone quarry. Trains only stopped here regularly from the Summer of 1965 in order to serve the Curraghs Wildlife Park, a newly-created attraction established by the IoM Government on the adjacent wetlands. During its first season the nameboard was lettered Ballavolley Halt for Wild Life Park, but from 1967 was known simply as Wild Life Park. With the park's protective fencing on the right, no.11 *Maitland* calls with a train from Douglas during July 1967. (D.J.Mitchell)

93.   The former gate-keepers lodge, which can also be seen on the left of the previous picture, is now in private hands. Today, the road only leads to the park entrance, which is just behind the photographer, the short piece of 3ft 0in gauge track being a reminder of the days when you could journey here by train. Within the grounds visitors can enjoy a wide range of animals and birds from many distant parts of the world in surrounds similar to their native habitats. In addition, the Manx Steam & Model Engineering Club operate 'The Orchid Line', a half-mile circuit of 5in and 7¼in dual gauge track which also incorporates a shorter 600ft length of rails set to a width of 3½in. A number of locomotives can often be seen in action, but perhaps the most relevant is a 5in gauge model of IoMR 2-4-0T no.6 *Peveril*. (T.Heavyside)

# SULBY GLEN

94. At first it was intended the station would be known as Sulby Siding, but when opened it was more appropriately named after the steep, winding glen that begins its spectacular ascent into the heart of the Northern Upland Massif from nearby. The glen itself has long been regarded as an important tourist attraction. The original station building was considered to be much too close to the track and, in 1910, was superseded by the structure seen in this eastward view on 19th August 1961. The raised platform also dates from 1910. On the right of the siding occupied by the M wagon is the goods platform and cattle pen. (J.L.Stevenson)

| Receipts | 1907 | 1917 | 1927 | 1937 | 1947 |
|---|---|---|---|---|---|
| Coaching | £546 | £378 | £723 | £374 | £1,348(a) |
| Goods | £102 | £83 | £138 | £13 | £86 |
| (a) Passenger £1,216, Parcels £132. | | | | | |

95. Here we take a closer look at the platform canopy. It was supported by six cast iron posts embellished with some ornate decorations. No.10 *G.H.Wood* has charge of a train from Ramsey on 14th August 1967. (A.M.Davies)

96. On the same day, the double 25ft-wide gates at the other end of the station have been swung across the A14 road, in readiness for this train to proceed on its journey to Ramsey. The A14 meanders from Jurby, near the coast, up Sulby Glen as far as the Bungalow station on the Snaefell Mountain Railway. The poster by the entrance shows the departure times of three trains in each direction and also declares 'It's Better By Rail!'. (A.M.Davies)

97. Later, the property was sold and converted into a house. A new outside wall was built near to the edge of the former platform, with a verandah formed over the front door by leaving part of the canopy and two of the original stanchions exposed, the remaining four supports being incorporated into the living quarters. It was photographed from the old trackbed on 19th May 2002. (T.Heavyside)

# SULBY BRIDGE

98.   The station took its name from the nearby bridge which carries the main A3 road from the south to Ramsey over the River Sulby. The road forms part of the circuit used for the famed TT (Tourist Trophy) motorcycle races. On 19th April 1950 a few passengers waiting by the slate-roofed, red sandstone station building, prepare to greet the arrival of a train from Douglas, the level crossing gates over the A17 Sulby to Bride road having already been opened. (H.C.Casserley)

| Receipts | 1907 | 1917 | 1927 | 1937 | 1947 |
|---|---|---|---|---|---|
| Coaching | £299 | £318 | £507 | £231 | £518(a) |
| Goods | £30 | £80 | £93 | £25 | £105 |
| (a) Passenger £460, Parcels £58. | | | | | |

99.   A second passenger's view from the carriage window of a passing train, this time looking back towards Douglas on 13th April 1960. At the end of the siding is cattle wagon no.K25. This was constructed by the IoMR in 1923 by utilising the spare chassis from MRCW coach no.B13 of 1873/74 vintage, when the body became part of newly-formed coach no.F60. Further along the siding is the cattle pen and loading dock. (J.L.Stevenson)

100.   The three-coach 3.25pm service from Douglas to Ramsey, led by no.8 *Fenella*, enters the loop and passes the goods siding on 19th August 1961. (J.L.Stevenson)

101.  As the crossing-keeper walks across to the far gates to reopen them to road traffic, no.10 *G.H.Wood* is seen from the cattle bank while on its way back to Douglas from Ramsey on 3rd June 1968. The siding had already been lifted. (D.J.Mitchell)

102.  The property was disposed of during the mid-1970s, the new owner carrying out some extensive renovations and improvements while making it suitable for use as a house. In honour of its past it is now known as *Railway House*, and was pictured from the adjacent roadway during May 2002. (T.Heavyside)

# LEZAYRE

103. The station, occasionally referred to as Garey, was situated in a rather isolated spot, and could be approached off either the A3 or A13 roads from Ramsey by way of a narrow lane which connects the two. From 1884 until 1926 there was a short siding on the north side of the running line. The station was downgraded to a 'request stop' in 1908, and while omitted from the timetables from September 1950 tickets continued to be issued until 1961, even after it officially ceased to be a 'request stop' in 1958! The stone building, complete with yellow brick quoins, is seen from the west on 22nd August 1961. (H.Stevenson)

| Receipts | 1942 | 1943 | 1945 | 1946 | 1947 |
|----------|------|------|------|------|------|
| Coaching | £15 | £21 | £14 | £7 | £3 |

Note: Returns only available for certain years during the 1940s. There were no receipts in respect of goods.

104. From 1967, under Lord Ailsa, the station was again listed in the timetables. In what proved to be its last month of usage, the twin-spectacle signal guarding the approach from Ramsey was recorded in September 1968. The semaphore was hand-operated by means of the lever near the foot of the post. The signal now forms part of a display by the water tower at Peel (see *Douglas to Peel* picture 120). A signal positioned on the far side of the station in respect of trains working in the opposite direction was removed during the early-1950s. The crossing-keepers cottage, now demolished, can be seen on the extreme left of the previous illustration.
(A.Matthewman/Breese Stamp Co)

105. After standing derelict for many years the station building was renovated during the 1990s and is now a private residence. A few lengths of rail mark the path of the former trackbed on 28th April 2001. (T.Heavyside)

# EAST OF LEZAYRE

106. The island's longest river, the Sulby, flows for 10½ miles from its source high in the Northern Upland Massif down to Ramsey. The Manx Northern rails were carried over the river near Ballakillingan by an 88ft-long wrought iron bowstring girder bridge. It was usually referred to as 'The Basket Bridge' on account of the arch-shaped stretcher tied above the centre line. Despite some strengthening work carried out by the IoMR in 1906, it was replaced by a lattice steel girder structure in 1914. Here no.5 *Mona* is about to step-off the 'new' bridge onto the south bank of the river with the 10.25am service from Douglas on 28th August 1961. (J.L.Stevenson)

107.  Looking towards Ramsey at Milntown crossing, on the outskirts of the town, in July 1968, we see the 12ft-wide gates provided over a minor road. The attendants lodge is on the left, while the line in the right foreground was installed only that year in order to facilitate the movement of oil from Peel to the 1960-opened Ramsey Power Station. The oil was transported in three ex-road tankers mounted on the underframes of former M wagons which had been specially adapted for the purpose (see *Douglas to Peel* picture 97). (A.M.Davies)

108.  The other end of the short, tightly-curved siding at Milntown lay within the confines of the electricity generating plant. The last consignment of oil to be brought in by rail was received a few days after this picture was taken on 22nd September 1968. The siding was removed in October 1969. (A.Matthewman/Breese Stamp Co)

# RAMSEY

X. Track plan in the days when the railway still served the harbour.

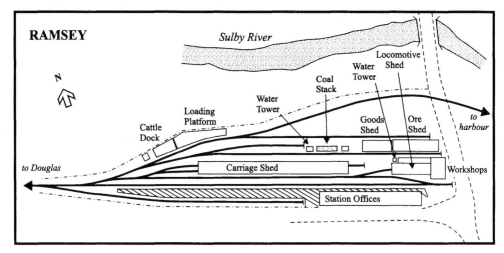

| Receipts | 1907 | 1917 | 1927 | 1937 | 1947 |
|---|---|---|---|---|---|
| Coaching | £2,185 | £2,142 | £2,475 | £2,266 | £2,570(a) |
| Goods | £966 | £1,095 | £1,257 | £508 | £1,375 |
| (a) Passenger £1,742, Parcels £828. | | | | | |

109. On then to our destination 'Royal' Ramsey, so called following the visits of King Edward VII and Queen Alexandra in 1902, and an earlier unscheduled call by Queen Victoria and her consort in 1847, although on the latter occasion only Prince Albert ventured ashore while Her Majesty rested on the royal yacht anchored in Ramsey Bay. Here, shortly after the turn of the century, no.1 *Ramsey*, one of the two 2-4-0Ts purchased by the MNR from Sharp Stewart in 1879, strides away with a mixed train for the south. Notice the Three Legs of Man, the symbol of the island, on the smokebox door. The station building, the headquarters of the Manx Northern Railway, is to the left of the rear wagon. (Manx National Heritage)

110. The crew pose by no.2 *Derby* before leaving with the 6.15pm to Douglas on 16th May 1927. The boiler is fitted with two Ross 'pop' safety valves, one positioned between the chimney and the bell-shaped dome with the other out of sight within the dome. *Derby* last ran in 1949, having completed 1,480,088 miles since new in 1873. It was subsequently dismantled in 1951, only the second IoMR Beyer Peacock 2-4-0T to suffer this fate. (A.W.Croughton/J.D.Darby Collection)

111. Six years later, in July 1933, the driver and fireman of no.3 *Pender* obligingly wait alongside the two-road corrugated iron carriage shed while the shutter is released. *Pender* has Salter safety valves. In 1951 it received the boiler seen in the previous picture from the withdrawn *Derby*, and then remained at work until 1959, by which time it had recorded 1,247,623 miles. In 1979 *Pender* was returned to Manchester, the city of its birth, and the next year became a sectionalised exhibit at the newly-opened Museum of Science & Industry. (H.C.Casserley)

112. In this scene, on a warm June day in 1939, two ladies walk jauntily along the platform towards the exit. The Beyer Peacock 2-4-0T, which had just brought in their train from Douglas, had already been unhooked and drawn forward prior to running round the stock. The timber canopy, which offered passengers some welcome protection from the elements on days of inclement weather, is seen to advantage. In the centre of the picture is the stone-built one-road engine shed, the nearest section having been added by the MNR in 1886 following the purchase of *Caledonia* the previous year. The workshop protrudes at the rear. To the left of the water tank, behind the G van, is the south wall of the ore and goods shed, while near the left-hand edge of the frame is the south-east corner of the carriage shed. (W.A.Camwell/Stephenson Locomotive Society)

113. Trains often departed from the bay platform on the south side of the station. On the same day as the previous picture, marshalled ready for the journey to Douglas are two carriages and five cattle wagons behind no.1 *Sutherland*. A second rake of stock stands by the main platform. (W.A.Camwell/Stephenson Locomotive Society)

⟶

114. The approach to the station was pictured on 25th August 1961. It will be noted that when the fish-tailed signal protecting the entry was in the 'off' position as here, there was no spectacle glass in front of the oil lamp. The ground levers which operated the points can be seen to the left of each set. (J.L.Stevenson)

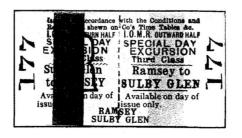

115. Covered vans nos G6 (on the left) and G12, former MNR no.15, await their next payloads outside the goods shed on 1st August 1962. The latter was manufactured by the Swansea Wagon Co in 1879, to which the MNR fitted a new ventilated body about the turn of the century, thus making it suitable for the movement of livestock as well as general goods. No.G6 was built by the Ashbury Carriage & Iron Co in 1877. Unladen the wagons each weighed approximately 3 tons and were designed to carry up to 6 tons. No.G6 was scrapped during the late-1970s while no.G12 has recently been restored by the IoMR. (J.L.Stevenson)

116. An uncluttered view of the north side of the layout from near the cattle dock in 1966, the year the railway remained closed. A second water tank stands between the tracks which served either side of the goods shed, the weighbridge being located on the track leading to the left-hand side. The water tank by the engine shed, seen in picture 112, is visible beyond the carriage shed on the right. The rails branching off on the far left once led to the harbour. (D.J.Mitchell)

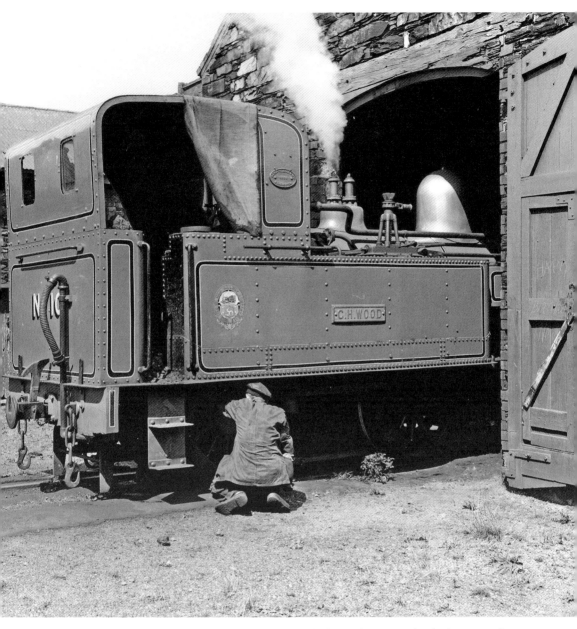

117. No.10 *G.H.Wood*, with its smokebox inside the shed, receives attention before returning to Douglas in July 1967. During the 1920s three engines were shedded here, but by the beginning of the 1960s only one was normally maintained at the shed. During the Ailsa regime none were left here overnight. (D.J.Mitchell)

118. To assess the viability of a car-carrying service an Austin Mini was transported from St John's on M wagon no.56 at the rear of a passenger train in September 1967. On arrival the wagon was shunted to the loading bank by no.10 *G.H.Wood* where the Manx-registered vehicle was driven off. The experiment was not repeated. (A.M.Davies)

119. The frontage of the cement-rendered station building had a distinct Italianate appearance. It was photographed from Station Road on 3rd September 1976 prior to demolition two years later in August 1978. The faded sign over what was once the entrance to the booking hall indicates the building had been used for a short time as a secondhand stores. The site depicted here is now occupied by Ramsey Bakery and the former approach area, to the left of the picture, by the Ramsey Town Commissioners Riverside Workshops. (D.Pearce)

# RAMSEY HARBOUR

120. Work on the harbour tramway from the goods yard across Bowring Road, then along Derby Road and the West Quay, began during the Summer of 1882, and the line was first used in December of that year. After the mining of lead ore had finished at Foxdale in 1911 the main traffic, albeit at times spasmodic, was imported coal, including that for use by the IoMR. It was last used in 1949. A section of the tramway at the east end had already been taken out of use back in 1924, and the remaining rails were lifted between 1955 and 1957 and the carriageway subsequently resurfaced. In happier times, with a trio of cyclists keeping pace and a photographer trying to outrun the train, no.1 *Sutherland* hauls four M wagons back towards the goods yard during August 1938. The swing bridge to be seen above the rear three wagons was opened in June 1892, and links the north and south banks of the River Sulby. It was manufactured by the Cleveland Bridge & Engineering Company of Darlington. (G.Harrop/J.D.Darby Collection)

121. We end our travels on the quayside on 25th October 2003, the harbour still being busy with both commercial vessels and pleasure craft. It is most regrettable that in reality it is no longer possible to sit back in a railway carriage and enjoy the ride from Douglas through to Ramsey behind one of the Beyer Peacock 2-4-0Ts or *Caledonia* as in days of yore, although as already noted it is feasible to walk most of the trackbed. As highlighted during our circuitous journey from the south, there remains much of interest along the way, and similarly Ramsey itself, as pictured here, is well worthy of a visit. Furthermore, on an even more positive note, if desired, Ramsey can still be reached by rail from Douglas by way of the Manx Electric Railway. (T.Heavyside)

# MP Middleton Press

**Easebourne Lane, Midhurst West Sussex. GU29 9AZ**

**OOP** Out of Print - Please check current availability  **BROCHURE AVAILABLE SHOWING NEW TITLES**
Tel:01730 813169   www.middletonpress.com   email:middletonpress.co.uk